DOMINATE
YOUR JOB
INTERVEW

ABOUT THE AUTHOR

Anatoly Volkhover is a dynamic thought leader and serial entrepreneur from Silicon Valley, who brings a background in mathematics, physics, and computer science, and a 30-year proven track record of technology innovation, mentorship, behavioral marketing, and brain research. He started using Neuro-Linguistic Programming (NLP) in his line of work more than a decade ago and honed his skills over years of extensive use. Recently, Anatoly has fostered a new startup initiative—ENEUM—which helps people unlock their full potential and open an entirely new chapter of their lives, through the use of proprietary brain stimulation technology. You can learn more about it on the company's website: **www.eneum.com**.

Anatoly has been on both sides of the job interview table countless times. He saw too often how a single nervous gesture, or a misplaced smile, or a poorly chosen body posture, negates all the experience and personal charm of the candidate. Anatoly thoroughly analyzed the mistakes made and the opportunities lost, as well as each individual success, and personally adopted, tested, and perfected the NLP techniques that ensure success. The best performing of those techniques form the foundation of this book.

ABOUT THE BOOK

This book is for anyone who is serious about landing their next job. It specifically focuses on gaining an unfair advantage in a face to face interview, over all other candidates that possess similar professional skills. This book will teach you how to prepare yourself, and how to subtly manipulate your interviewers, to make YOU the candidate of choice—in many cases, deeply on the subconscious level—by applying techniques of Neuro-Linguistic Programming (NLP). Until recently, these techniques have only been employed in secret by psychologists, politicians, and spies. The purpose of this book is to place those techniques into YOUR hands and make them an instrument for achieving success.

The book is short enough to be read in a few hours. It is also densely packed with advice. Read it with focus, do the recommended exercises, and come to your next job interview fully equipped to win.

Best of luck!

DOMINATE
YOUR JOB
INTERVIEW

CREATE AN UNFAIR ADVANTAGE WITH
30 POWERFUL NLP TECHNIQUES

ANATOLY VOLKHOVER

TAKE CONTROL WITH
MANIPULATION TECHNIQUES
EMPLOYED BY LEADING SPY AGENCIES.

TABLE OF CONTENTS

FOREWORD

Things are going great. You applied for the job of your dreams, passed the initial phone screening, and are heading for the on-site interview tomorrow. You know the subject matter well and aren't afraid of questions. Still, you are nervous, and rightfully so—there are many candidates being interviewed for this position, and the employer will select only one. What are your chances?

Throughout my 30-year-long career, I was on both sides of the interview table. Based on those experiences, I would argue the following applies in nearly every hiring case: **your skills are not the main determining factor in landing a job**. How so, you may ask? Well, one typically applies for a job that matches their existing skillset. If your skills don't match those required for the open position, then you wouldn't get to the interview in the first place. Or, if you lie on your resume, you will be likely eliminated during the very first phone screen. Which means that if you are going to an interview, then your skills are on par with what's required, and there is also a high likelihood that the employer is considering several contenders with a similar if not identical set of skills. Who will they pick? They will hire the person they like on a personal level; someone they think will be easy and pleasant to work with. Thus, assuming that you are already a subject matter expert, your chances of getting the job directly depend on how well you present yourself as a *person*. The purpose of this book is to help you with that, through the use of NLP.

What is NLP? It stands for Neuro-Linguistic Programming. It was created by Richard Bandler and John Grinder way back in the 1970s, and then further developed by generations of psychologists, coaches, and hypnotherapists. NLP studies the structure of interpersonal communications, including both the spoken language and the subliminal language of our bodies, and provides us with effective tools for influencing others beyond words, on the subliminal level. Unsurprisingly, NLP quickly became a part of every spy agency's training program, is taught in hard negotiation courses, and has been widely adopted by political speechwriters and coaches. BTW, one of the most renowned life coaches—Anthony Robbins—is a former student of John Grinder, one of NLP's founding fathers.

This book is not a textbook on NLP. There is great material out there that can help you learn NLP from the ground up, but such in-depth study would require time and dedication. This book focuses squarely on helping you to win the next interview and land your dream job. I tried hard to make it as concise as possible, focusing on making it useful even if you get the book just a day before your scheduled interview. For those reasons, the NLP techniques are explained in layman's terms, bypassing all the specialized jargon, and without dwelling much on the underlying psychological and biological principles. I also limited the NLP techniques to those 30 that can be learned quickly. I will do my best to explain the psychological and physiological underpinnings of the techniques whenever it fits in a few sentences; in more complex cases, you will have to trust my extensive experience as an NLP practitioner.

While writing this book, I was very careful to make the material useful for any profession, any pay grade, and any gender identity. It is intended to be equally helpful to seasoned professionals, college graduates, and school dropouts alike.

Now that we clarified what this book is, and what it is not, let's dive straight in.

CHAPTER

1

LOOKS VS. SUBSTANCE

On the evening of September 26, 1960, in Chicago, Illinois, a presidential debate occurred that changed the nature of national politics. On that day, John F. Kennedy and Richard Nixon squared off in the first televised presidential debate in American history. Prior to 1960, the voters rarely saw the candidates in person. They saw their pictures in the newspapers and heard them on the radio.

The story has it that those Americans who tuned in over the radio tended to think Nixon had won the debates. His fiery speech was well written and flawlessly delivered. However, those who watched the debates on TV reacted very differently. They saw a tired Nixon, wearing an ill-fitting shirt, still recovering from two weeks in the hospital after his knee injury, his gaze drifting about the room, sweaty and pale. They also saw a tanned and fit John Kennedy, after a few weeks of campaigning in California, never breaking eye contact with the camera, radiating confidence. The whooping TV audience of 70 million had given Kennedy a clear win, despite his apparent lack of experience. Six weeks later, JFK won the election.

The Kennedy-Nixon debates had a chilling effect on politicians. The next live televised presidential debate did not occur for another decade and a half. Risk-averse candidates worried about looks winning over substance, and rightfully so. Body language is much harder to control than spoken words. It takes years of dedicated training to fully master. And it takes only a minor disconnect between the body and the spoken language to permanently lose the trust of an audience.

How is this story relevant to your upcoming interview?

Trust is the most important currency in interpersonal communications. If the interviewer trusts you to fit well into the team, they will hire you. But how do you establish trust when you are just meeting the person for the first time in your life?

We all unconsciously decide if we trust someone at first sight (or not). The underlying mechanisms have very little to do with logic; they are pure biology and psychology. Research shows that our decision to trust or distrust a person is 55% based on their body language, 38% on their voice and manner of speaking, and only 7% on what they are actually saying. Which is great news—because you can score a win even before you say hello, just by walking in the right way.

This is what this book is about—how to condition yourself, and how to manipulate the interviewer's perception of you, to maximize the positive outcome.

Let's get started.

CHAPTER

2

SCREENING CALL

The screening call is usually performed by an HR person, but in smaller companies, it is done by the hiring manager. This is your chance to gather actionable intelligence and better prepare.

TECHNIQUE 01: COLLECT INTEL

Go over the company's website and try to find out as much as you can about the company and its product and services. If you cannot figure some of it out, don't hesitate to ask.

On the call, show genuine interest in what the company does. Use what you gathered from the website, to show that you've done your homework, and you are seriously interested.

Use the screening call as an opportunity to learn more about the open position, the challenges, the skills required, and why the position opened up in the first place. Some of the most common reasons might be:

- Backfill for someone who left the company

- Backfill for someone who wasn't performing well
- General growth of the company
- Newly required skills

Knowing more about the opening allows you to position yourself better at the interview, by matching exactly what the company needs.

Also, ask who will be interviewing you. Write down their names, positions, and (!) proper pronunciations. Afterward, research them as described further in the Homework chapter.

TECHNIQUE 02: COMPANY'S HR IS YOUR BEST FRIEND

Contrary to what you might think, the HR rep on the phone with you is your best friend. Their performance is gauged by how quickly they can fill the position, and with the quality of the candidates. Thus, it is in their interest to see you pass the interview with flying colors. Use this to your advantage, and don't hesitate to ask questions. You can even ask for whatever recommendations they can give you for the upcoming interview—no matter how little they give you, it will be golden.

Do not confuse the HR rep with an external hiring agent. The latter is not a part of the organization, and they usually know little to nothing about the company. In many cases, they are just interested in corralling as many candidates for the position as possible, in the hope that one of them will pass. You will get no useful information from those folks. Don't hate them for this—if they get you in the door, it counts.

TECHNIQUE 03: REACH CLARITY ON COMPENSATION BAND

When the employer lists no specific compensation for the job, it means they would rather not disclose their budget for this position, hoping to get you cheaper. But it also means that their budget may be below one you would ever consider—so why waste your time and theirs? Ask them right there on the screening call about the compensation band they have in mind. If the person on another side of the line has even half a brain, then they will turn around and ask what you are looking for. Be prepared to give them the lower end of your band, keeping the upper end open. For instance, you can use your current salary as a reference point, like this: "I am currently making $70,000 a year—and I expect to be making substantially more at the new job to make the move interesting." If your job application asked you about your current compensation, then you may consider this step already executed— because you already told the employer your rock bottom price. If you have no current compensation to use as a reference, then come up with a number that will make you happy if you take the job. If this is your first job, and you have no reference points to come up with the number, figure out how much you would need to be making after tax to live on

your own, pay rent, and cover all the expenses—
and then name the before tax figure that will at least
afford you the lifestyle you seek.

CHAPTER

3

HOMEWORK

Having the names of the interviewers will help you prepare. Here is how.

TECHNIQUE 04: NAMES AND ICE BREAKERS

Research the interviewer(s) on LinkedIn, and potentially other social networks. See if you have something in common. For example, places they worked at previously, or the school they went to (your dad or brother or wife might have worked at the same place—ask them if they ever met). You may see a photo of a dog or a cat on the interviewer's profile, which will make a great conversational topic if you also have a dog or a cat. Be authentic, don't make up an imaginary dog. But if you have one, it would not hurt to say "I noticed a super-cute looking doodle on your LinkedIn profile—I have a dog myself—do you guys ever bring dogs to the office here?" This is a great ice breaker. Clearly, there are numerous other topics you can consider using as an ice breaker. Commit the details to memory and use them during the interview.

TECHNIQUE 05: PREPARE YOURSELF MENTALLY

From each interviewer's profile, grab their photo. For each of the interviewers, visualize yourself speaking with them about things unrelated to interview—like you would chitchat with a friend. Here is how. Sit comfortably in front of a switched off TV. Close your eyes. Imagine watching a video that features you and that person speaking. Make sure you see a clear picture and hear the sound. Visualize talking about weather, food, dogs, vacation plans—any positive subjects. Mentally speak with those people as if you have been working at the company for a few weeks or even months. Make this visualization a routine at least once a day, for each day leading up to the interview.

This will train your subconsciousness to be around those people and to react positively and without stress when you see them. In this way, you will no longer feel as if you are among strangers at the interview.

TECHNIQUE 06: IF YOU ARE UNCERTAIN

If you lack some of the expertise that the position lists as required or desired, and are worried that you will be questioned about it, do the following. Sit comfortably in front of a switched off TV. Close your eyes. Imagine that the TV plays a video recording of your interview with one of the interviewers you researched, and they ask you exactly the question you fear to fail at. Imagine that you have a remote control with the knobs controlling volume, color saturation, and brightness. While visualizing the uncomfortable scenes from your upcoming interview, mentally twist the volume knob to turn the volume down to an inaudible level. Then use the color saturation knob to make the colors dull, all the way to gray. Then use the brightness knob to slowly reduce brightness until it is a completely dark screen. Open your eyes to see the real dark screen in front of you. If you ever feel any residual discomfort about that episode, repeat the procedure. Repeat this technique for every interview question that you fear.

If you are curious to learn how such visualization techniques work, read through Appendix II: How Visualizations Work.

CHAPTER

4

RIGHT BEFORE THE INTERVIEW

There are several things you can do right before the interview to improve your chances of success. They are mainly related to getting relaxed and into the right mood.

TECHNIQUE 07: DRESS CODE

Ahead of time, figure out what is the dress code in the company you are interviewing for. Dress respectfully, but don't overdo it. In other words, if everyone in the company wears shorts to work, then wear jeans, but don't pull the suit and tie stunt.

Make sure that whatever clothing you plan to wear, it will keep you comfortable for the duration of the interview. For instance, if high heels give you blisters, then swap them for flats or loafers. Consider the weather, the temperature, and the duration of the interview. Any discomfort from poorly chosen clothing will likely be misinterpreted as insecurity or as if you are hiding something.

TECHNIQUE 08: CALM DOWN

It is important that you go into the interview confidently. You want to avoid being stressed. There are many ways of achieving that, but here is the easiest: have some comfort food. Don't overeat, but have something that you consider pleasant and comforting. Many of us carry those foods all the way from childhood. Have some of that. There are a few ingredients to avoid though—garlic, onions, bacon, and any other foods that make your breath smell. You never know the reaction the interviewer might have to a strong smell; what's comfortable for you is not necessarily comfortable for them. Avoid any kind of alcoholic beverages, try to refrain from smoking. Oh, and no coffee if you can.

If you are interested in how this works, refer to Appendix III: Why Eating Calms You Down.

TECHNIQUE 09: BUILD UP SELF-ESTEEM

This is especially important if this is your first interview, or if you are simply nervous and unsure of your ability to pass. Take a sheet of paper and a pen. Then write down all the things that you do really well—not just professionally, but literally *everything*, from cooking to riding a bicycle. If you have less than half a page, keep going, rack your brain—there has to be more. Once your page is filled up, look at it, and reflect on how many skills you have actually mastered. This will help.

TECHNIQUE 10: DON'T BE LATE

Give yourself enough time to get to the interview ahead of schedule. You will need 10+ minutes to do the exercises outlined below, and you also want to give yourself more wiggle room to compensate for unexpected traffic, lack of parking nearby, etc. If you give yourself an extra half an hour, that will be plenty.

TECHNIQUE 11: GET INTO A POSITIVE MOOD

The moment you walk in, you will be subconsciously evaluated by the interviewer. For the lack of other data points, they will rely primarily on their subconscious evaluation. If they perceive you positively, they will be biased in your favor throughout the entire interview process and will provide you all the help they can.

Here is the technique that will help you get in the right mood. For 5-10 minutes, recall the most pleasant moments in your life. Replay them in your memory, to the extent that you feel the emotions in your body physically. Spread your arms wide, tilt your head back, and continue recalling the good memories until you feel that a wide uncontrollable smile has formed on your face. Then walk in and meet the interviewer.

Try to maintain the same happy mood throughout the interview. If you are meeting with multiple interviewers, use small breaks in between to get back into a happy mood.

CHAPTER

5

AT THE INTERVIEW

MEMORIZE YOUR ARRIVAL

Memorize how you arrive, everything from parking your car, or exiting an Uber, or getting off the bus, to walking up to the employer's building, to entering the door, to meeting someone at the front desk. Memorize not only the visuals but your sensory input—the steps, the smells in the air, the street noise, the weather outside—sun or the rain, the temperature, etc. Make sure to commit it all to memory; you will need it later for Technique 27.

TECHNIQUE 12: TAKE THE WATER

If offered the water, take it. If offered choices, take plain non-carbonated water. Say thank you. People enjoy being helpful. Let them, even if you are not thirsty.

If also offered food at lunchtime, express both genuine surprise and appreciation, and smile widely. Be careful with food—don't make a mess of yourself.

TECHNIQUE 13: CALL THE INTERVIEWER BY NAME, AND USE THE ICE BREAKER

If you did your homework, then you know who is interviewing you, and how to properly pronounce their names. Use it. There is nothing better sounding to a person than their own name. Use their name throughout the interview, as often as reasonable. The interviewer will love you for this.

If you prepared an ice breaker (see homework from Technique 04), use it immediately upon introduction.

TECHNIQUE 14: MAINTAIN OPTIMAL DISTANCE

Maintain the optimal distance from the interviewer. Generally speaking, our subconsciousness interprets distances as follows.

Intimate Distance 6-8 inches	Close relationship or greater comfort between individuals. It occurs between best friends, parent and child, and lovers.
Personal Distance 1.5-4 feet	It occurs between friends, sometimes between family members.
Social Distance 4-12 feet	This is where a person's acquaintances are located. Coworkers, gym buddies, classmates, yoga buddies.

Public Distance 12-25 feet	This is the distance for public speaking

You should try to place yourself at the outer end of the Personal Distance range, from the interviewer, i.e., within 3-4 feet from them. Do not inch into the Intimate Distance to avoid discomfort on both sides.

TECHNIQUE 15: HOW TO ORIENT YOURSELF

When you are sitting down with the interviewer, try to avoid sitting face to face. In nature, a face to face stance indicates opposition and threat, triggering the *fight or flight reflex*. We subconsciously consider a person who is standing or sitting in front of us as an adversary, unless of course, we have known that person for a while already. The best way is to position yourself at an angle to the interviewer so that you can still conveniently see each other without straining your necks, but not face to face. If you are offered a seat across a desk, you can put your chair slightly at an angle to the desk, for the same result.

TECHNIQUE 16: CREATE PERSONAL SPACE

In nature, larger animals enjoy more respect. This behavior is biologically wired into humans as well. The more space you occupy, the more respect you generally get on the first encounter. Your space refers not only to your body but to your belongings—your phone, notepad, purse, bag, printed copy of your resume, etc. When sitting down for an interview, claim as much space as you can, up to 50% of the entire space available on the desk, by surrounding yourself with your "stuff." It should be well organized, and it will earn you two score points at once—both for being well organized and for being "larger" than the other contenders.

TECHNIQUE 17: AVOID INTERRUPTIONS

You don't want to be interrupted during the interview. Switch your phone off. Don't just put it in silent mode—switch it off, completely. Same for your smartwatch—turn it off. Leave home or secure all the noise-making items (bracelets, keys, etc.). Don't fiddle with the contents of your pockets. Do not let an unexpected sound get in the way of you and your dream job.

TECHNIQUE 18: BODY LANGUAGE

Your body is likely to give away your thoughts and feelings even if you don't know it. There are a few simple rules to follow, to convey only positive information. Sit upright, lean forward when the interviewer expects to have your full attention. Never cross your arms or legs, or lock your feet around the leg of the chair. Don't touch your upper body—especially your hair, face, or clothing. Do not cover your mouth. Do not lock your fingers. Show upward open palms as a subliminal sign of openness.

There is a lot of research behind all of this. If you are interested in learning more about common body language, and using it more appropriately—and also learning to read your interviewer—refer to Appendix I: Common Body Language.

TECHNIQUE 19: MAINTAIN EYE CONTACT AND SMILE

Eye contact should not be a continuous unblinking stare—but you need to re-establish eye contact with the interviewer before you start speaking again. You can (and should) take your eyes off them to write down your notes, or to do an exercise if offered, but once done—always find the interviewer's eyes before starting to speak. Once the eye contact is re-established, smile, and then talk.

TECHNIQUE 20: MIRROR THE POSTURE AND SPEECH OF THE INTERVIEWER

We tend to blindly trust people that act similarly to us. Thus, to develop trust with the interviewer, try to mirror their actions.

Start with mirroring their body posture; sit the same way they do. Do not make them suspect you are imitating them; wait for about 20 seconds before adjusting your own posture in response. The interviewer leaned back on their chair; you follow with the same. They put their hands behind the back of the head; you do the same. They placed their hands on the desk in front of them; you follow.

The next thing to mirror is the interviewer's speech—adjust yours to match the loudness, the speed of delivery, and the pauses.

It is important to stay authentic while mirroring someone. Experiment in advance on unsuspecting friends—if you do everything right, they should not notice, but may warm up to you more than usual.

TECHNIQUE 21: MATCH THE INTERVIEWER'S PREFERRED COMMUNICATION STYLE

People perceive things differently. Some prefer to see a picture—they are called *visual* communicators. Others prefer hearing about the subject matter—we call them *auditory* communicators. Some prefer written words—those are *read/write* personalities. Finally, there are people that prefer tactile and other sensory input (pressure, temperature, density, weight, force, etc.). If you can figure out which type is your interviewer, then you can deliver your story in a way that will be perceived in the most optimal way.

Sometimes the interviewer's communication style is obvious. For instance, if they immediately start drawing diagrams on a whiteboard—they are the visual type. If they write something on a pad and hand it to you to read—they are read/write. In less obvious cases, you can detect the interviewer's communication style by carefully listening to how they construct their phrases. The table below shows some examples, although they are far from being exhaustive.

If the interviewer says...	Then they are...
I see... Imagine if... Picture this... Show me...	Visual
I hear... Tell me... It sounds like...	Auditory
Write this... Read that...	Read/Write
I feel... I sense...	Kinesthetic

Why is it important to understand the communication style of the interviewer? Because you can use it to your advantage, by delivering the information in their preferred way. For a visual person, use a whiteboard or hand-drawn pictures. If not available, use phrases like "Imagine this..." or "Picture this...." For a read/write person, try to put your answers on paper *as text*. For auditory, use phrases like "Let me tell you how..." or "How does that sound?" For kinesthetic, use phrases like "How would this make you feel?"

Don't limit your creativity by the above examples. For instance, when discussing communications, you may refer to them as "discussions" or "talks" for an auditory type, but "messages" for read/write, and "touchpoints" for kinesthetic.

TECHNIQUE 22: STAY CALM

Maintain a friendly calm demeanor throughout the interview. Sometimes, however, this can be hard—you may get nervous or stressed. If that happens, use the Disassociation technique described here. You may need to try it a few times in advance, to get the hang of it.

So here are you, sitting at the interview, nervous and overstressed. Mentally, step out of your body from the back, and take a couple of steps backward. You mentally should see your own back in front of you. You look at yourself, and you fully understand that person (you), the cause of the stress, and you can also see the entire room and the interviewer. You who stepped out are not stressed or nervous, you are just an observer who can see and think clearly. You evaluate the situation, you calmly decide on the best course of action, and then you step back into your own body, knowing exactly what needs to be done. You transfer your entire calm state of mind to the nervous version of self and continue with the interview.

Repeat as needed.

TECHNIQUE 23: DON'T LIE

There are several reasons to never lie in an interview.

First, your body will likely give you away. This comes from our childhood "programming"—we were all told that a lie will lead to a punishment, and we start showing the common signs of stress and fear: covering eyes and/or ears, rubbing eyelids, looking away, not invoking the usual gesticulation, touching our upper body, adjusting clothing. An experienced interviewer will know you are lying; an inexperienced will get a general sense that you are hiding something or are just being extremely nervous.

So unless you have taken the classes on how to pass a polygraph test, just don't lie.

TECHNIQUE 24: DON'T BS YOUR WAY THROUGH

If you don't know the answer to the question being asked, don't try to BS your way through. There are several reasons for that:

- A wrong answer scores lower than no answer
- You will have a chance to explain why you don't have this particular expertise
- By wasting time on BS, you are taking time away from the next question which you could have answered perfectly

- Admitting a lack of knowledge in a particular area will earn you a reputation as a straight shooter

Tell the interviewer that you would like to research this later today, and follow up later. Ask for the interviewer's email so that you can send them your answer. Write down the question, research it thoroughly after the interview, and send a thank you email to the interviewer with the question and answer included. Make sure to do it on the same day (many companies demand that interviewers publish their interview notes internally the same day or early next, and the sooner you send the right answer, the higher the chance that it will make a difference).

TECHNIQUE 25: PREPARE THE ANSWERS TO TYPICAL QUESTIONS

There are several questions that are universally asked during the interview. You should prepare your answers in advance. Here are a few examples for you to consider.

Why are you interested in our company?

Connect your answer to what you like about the company's products or services. One of the universal answers is that you are *looking for an ideal place to fully unlock your potential, and you believe that this is the place*. If you are interviewing for a famous company, say Apple Computers, then you can say that *it was your dream from childhood to work for Apple*. Careful there—people will know that you are being dishonest if the company has two employees, operates out of a garage, and was founded three months ago.

Under no circumstances should you say that you are simply looking for higher compensation, even if that is your true motivation. People just don't like that. You can mention it as a secondary goal, if you like.

Why do you want to leave your current employer?

The answer to this should be well-coordinated with the previous question. For instance, if you name unlocking your full potential as the primary criteria for you looking for a new job, then the reason why you want to leave the current employer should be that you have reached the ceiling there in terms of how you can apply yourself.

Never say that the current employer underpays you, this may backfire. Never criticize your current employer, always speak respectfully about it.

Will long commute be a problem?

This is asked frequently if you live far away from the office. An exhausting commute is a big resignation driver in urban areas, and the company wouldn't want to hire someone who is statistically a high flight risk. If your commute will indeed be inconvenient, then you should be fully prepared to answer this question.

You may dismiss the question with a smile, admitting that you can use some time on the train to catch up on unread books. You might be planning to move closer—which is great news for the employer, a person who lives next door will likely stay with the company longer. Don't attempt to dismiss a question with a simple "not a problem," as the commute will remain a red flag attached to your candidacy.

CHAPTER

6

AFTER THE INTERVIEW

The interview might be over, but you are not done yet. There are still a few things you need to do. Read on.

TECHNIQUE 26: IF YOU FEEL BAD

If you have a sinking feeling about any part of the interview, use the following technique to alleviate it. It is important as you will otherwise be mentally coming back to it over and over again, and this may create a mental block that negatively impacts your future interviews. This technique will prevent it and will make you feel better.

Sit comfortably in front of a switched off TV. Close your eyes. Imagine that the TV shows the part of the interview that went wrong. Imagine that you have a remote control with the knobs controlling volume, color saturation, and brightness. While re-watching your interview, mentally twist the volume knob to turn the volume down to an inaudible level. Then use the color saturation knob to make the colors dull, all the way to gray. Then use the brightness knob to slowly reduce brightness until it is a completely dark screen. Open your eyes to see the real dark screen in front of you. If you ever feel any residual discomfort about that episode, repeat the procedure. Repeat the process for every uncomfortable memory from the interview.

TECHNIQUE 27: PREPARE FOR THE FUTURE

Remember how you memorized your arrival to the employer's office right before the interview? We will need this now. Sit comfortably in front of a switched off TV. Close your eyes. Imagine that the TV shows a calendar counting the dates to your desired employment date—two weeks from now (feel free to adjust as needed). Once the calendar shows the date of your employment, it fades away and gets replaced with the visualization of your arrival to the office. It is all exactly as it was when you went for the interview—you see yourself taking every step, and sense the same smells, breathe the same air—with one exception: you definitively know that this time, you are going in for your first day at a new job.

Replay it a couple of times, and make sure it feels as if everything is happening to you for real.

Then STOP THINKING ABOUT THE INTERVIEW COMPLETELY. Don't bring it up in memory until you get a follow-up call or email. You are done with this interview, so turn the page and move on. A good way to switch your attention to something else is physical exercise.

CHAPTER

7

FOLLOW-UP CALL

Someone from HR or the hiring manager will usually email you if you have failed, or they will call you in person if they have decided to move forward with you. They will want to let you know personally that the company is going to extend an offer to you, and when to expect it. They will usually mention the proposed terms, such as title, compensation, signing bonus, stock allocation, performance bonus, health benefits, 401K benefits, etc. In sales jargon, this is a "closing," and the HR person on the line with you is a "salesperson," and you are the "customer." The tables have turned, it's no longer you selling yourself—the company wants to hire you, and you can use this to negotiate a better deal.

Many interpret the forthcoming offer as a "take-it-or-leave-it" deal, but this can't be further from the truth. In fact, the larger the company, the more red tape needs to be dealt with before getting the offer approved. For a hiring HR person, getting a "no" to an offer that went out means a highly visible failure. This is why they are calling you in advance, to make sure you understand the terms and agree to them verbally. So if you want to negotiate, this is a perfect time. Don't expect an immediate yes/no answer, they will need to go back, discuss, and pre-approve—which they will, and they will call you back. The worst that can happen is that they will stick to their original offer, but more often than not some concessions will be made.

Besides negotiating the straight salary compensation, you may also consider a Signing Bonus, a Performance Bonus, and other perks—as explained below.

TECHNIQUE 28: SIGNING BONUS

Signing Bonus is an interesting instrument that works both in your and the employer's favor. It is a one-time payment, usually included with your first paycheck, for a pre-negotiated amount. You will have to sign a paper that will explain that the signing bonus must be repaid if you leave the company of your own volition within a year of your start date at work. After a year, you are free to leave at any time, with no repayments. In other words, it incentivizes you to join the company, and it locks you in for a year—an interesting mutually beneficial instrument, frequently used in the high tech industry. What's interesting is that signing bonuses are sometimes easier to approve as one-time payments than an increase of a recurring compensation.

Example:

You are asking for $80,000 annual compensation. The company has an internal policy that puts a person of your experience in the $60,000-$70,000 pay band, so they can't give you the $80,000 you are seeking as salary. But they might be able to give you a $70,000 salary + $10,000 signing bonus, which will also "lock" you for a year. They also understand that they will have to raise your compensation by $10,000 minimum in the next 12 months, or you will likely leave. In a year, they will definitely know if you are worth the additional expense, and will act accordingly. For most companies, keeping a person who performs well is far more cost-effective than training a new one.

If you are negotiating your salary with the company, and they are telling you that they have reached their upper limit, you may suggest a signing bonus yourself. There is a chance they have not thought of it, especially if the company is not in high-tech space.

TECHNIQUE 29: PERFORMANCE BONUS

Performance bonus is typically a discretionary bonus paid annually, based on how the company performed and how you performed, relative to the expectations. Performance bonuses are usually expressed as a percentage of your salary comp. For instance, a 10% performance bonus on a salary of $80,000 means that the maximum bonus amount is $8,000.

Sometimes you can negotiate a performance bonus. Your sales pitch for that would be grounded in your performance. You say: "I know that you will be ecstatic about my performance once you hire me. I also understand that you have no proof of my performance at this point. For that reason, let's consider an annual 10% performance bonus. We will jointly set the goals for my first year with my manager, and I get the bonus proportionate to my achievements towards the set goals."

TECHNIQUE 30: OTHER PERKS

Besides monetary benefits, you can also negotiate other perks. For instance, one day a week of remote work, if your work can be done from home, and you enjoy working remotely. Or it could be a custom schedule, which allows you to beat the traffic.

If you made vacation plans, don't forget to mention them as a part of the negotiation—you need to negotiate additional days credited to your vacation balance before you get the chance to earn them.

CHAPTER

8

THE OFFER

The offer usually carries an expiration date, many limit you to 48 hours, sometimes shorter. By the time you get it, you should already know if you want the job, and the terms were discussed over the phone. So the only thing you need to do is to make sure that the terms you verbally agreed to are properly reflected on paper. People do make mistakes, and it is in your interest to make sure you are fully on board with the terms of the offer. If you have any questions, you should not hesitate to call the company and ask. If you see an error, don't jump to conclusions—most likely, no evil intent is involved, could be a simple human error. They will correct the errors and will send you another copy to sign.

That's it—once signed, you have your dream job. Congratulations!

AFTERWORD

While writing this book, I was torn between the desire to make it small and digestible in a short period of time, and the itch to tell you more about NLP, explain in further detail every recommendation, and give you more techniques. I included the common body language for those hungry for more in Appendix I. Unfortunately, all of the more advanced techniques required some degree of repetitive training, and I talked myself out of including them.

Instead, I'd like to recommend a mobile app to you. The app will help you stay calm and positive throughout the entire job search process, will assist with keeping your energy levels high, and will ensure that you sleep better at night. It can also help with the adaptation process once you have landed the new job, especially if you will be performing intellectually challenging work, or will work in a team, or will manage others, or if you will be working in sales.

The name of the app is ENEUM, and you can learn more about the science behind it from https://www.eneum.com.

As one of ENEUM's founders and its primary architect, I can tell you that many of the NLP techniques that did not make into this book due to their complexity are leveraged in the ENEUM's mobile app, with 10x efficiency, thanks to the use of technology that effectively replaces complex visualizations. You might want to check it out. Visit https://www.eneum.com or search for ENEUM directly in Apple's App Store or in Google Play.

For the purposes of job search and for quick and easy adaptation to the new job, look for packages called SOS and Business. For those going after a technology or research job, you may also want to consider the package called Mind.

I HOPE THIS BOOK COMES IN HANDY WHEN YOU HEAD OUT FOR YOUR NEXT INTERVIEW . . . AND THE NEXT, AND THE NEXT. BEST OF LUCK WITH YOUR JOB SEARCH, AND WITH LANDING THE JOB OF YOUR DREAMS—WITH A KILLER $$ COMP!

My very best,
Anatoly Volkhover

P.S. I am always looking for ways to improve. This book is no exception. I am very much interested in receiving your feedback—what worked well for you, what didn't, and why. I'd like to encourage you to leave your honest review on Amazon. This will help not only me, but also other readers to understand if this book is a good source for them.

APPENDIX I
COMMON BODY LANGUAGE

There are common elements of body language that we encounter every day, and frequently read and use ourselves without realizing it. If you want to communicate on a subliminal level during your interview, or clearly read the reaction of the interviewer, then refer to the Positive and Negative tables below.

POSITIVE BODY LANGUAGE

This is the body language you should be using. If you have the time, learn it, and your communications will become much more effective, way beyond the context of an interview.

Also, recognize those gestures as a positive sign when used by your interviewer.

Shoulder Shrug	Shows that a person does not understand what you are talking about. Sometimes, it also indicates doubt and disagreement.
Ring OK Sign Thumbs Up	Indicates the correctness of what you are saying.

Both hands raised upward, palms facing forward	Indicates a warm welcome and receptiveness to what you are saying.
Rubbing hands	Indicates that a person has positive expectations for the ongoing activities
Steepling hands	Shows confidence. When used by the interviewer, it may signal scrutiny. It could mean that a person is assessing you or observing you thoroughly.
Collapsed or relaxed hands	Indicate comfort and neutrality in nature.
Touching the cheek and jaw using the fingers	Indicates evaluation and criticism.
Arm gripping	Done by someone who wants to make their presence felt by the people around.
Leaning posture	Indicates an easygoing and relaxed attitude. Shows possessiveness and ownership.

NEGATIVE BODY LANGUAGE

This is the body language that you want to avoid at an interview. It may come in handy in other contexts, but for the interview those gestures may have a negative impact.

If used by your interviewer, use the interpretations below to understand what their body is telling you, and adjust quickly.

Pointing finger	Emphasizing the point calls to your personal attention if pointed at you.
Clenched hands	Frequently employed by people who are difficult to decipher.
Gripping hands	Indicates fear, pain, frustration, or anger.
Arms crossed	Indicates that the person is unopen to the communicated information. Sometimes indicates a negative attitude and defensiveness. When uncrossed, it indicates an openness to suggestions and receptiveness.
Hands in the front pocket while	Indicates aggressiveness and dominance. It also

showing the thumbs	connotes negative behavior and superior attitude.
Mouthguard (clamping mouth with a hand)	Indicates censorship of one's words. It is possible that they want to say something, but unsure if that's a good idea.
Rubbing or scratching the head	Indicates a person who is confused, having self-doubts, or finding it hard to decide or think.
Collar pull	Indicates anger, frustration, or stress.
Holding the head using the palms	Indicates boredom and unreceptiveness to details.
Arm gripping	Done by someone who wants to make their presence felt by the people around.
Hands on waist	Often indicates readiness, but with a hint of aggression.
Crossed legs	Shows nervousness, anxiety, and defensiveness.
Feet locked around the leg of the chair	Indicates tough-mindedness and stubbornness.

APPENDIX II
HOW VISUALIZATIONS WORK

Several techniques in this book are based on so-called visualizations. In the process, you visualize a TV screen playing either highly desired imaginary outcomes or undesired real or imaginary events. Since those techniques may seem a bit unusual, I decided to explain them here.

When dealing with desired outcomes, visualization prepares your subconscious to accept them as if they already happened.

Every time you consciously think of something, your subconscious controls the rest of your functions. Ever driven a car for half an hour, lost in thought, and then realized that you arrived but have no recollection of how you actually drove all the way? Your subconscious was in the driver's seat. It was reading the road signs, watching the traffic lights, avoided collisions with other cars, while keeping your lungs breathing, your heart beating, etc. In other words, your subconscious is a supercomputer that is in control of no less than 95% of your actions. BTW, it controls your body language too, unless you consciously intervene.

Now, if your subconscious is controlling so many functions, then you must "program" it to help you win the interview, otherwise it is clueless, and may act of its own accord. Unfortunately, the subconscious does not understand verbal or written commands very well. Instead, it responds to so-called *modalities*, or internal representations of our *senses*—such as visual, auditory, kinesthetic, olfactory, gustatory, plus our "internal dialogue." In other words, it subconsciously learns through pictures, movements, voices, etc. We can "program" our subconscious by mentally feeding it input in the form of those modalities—for instance, visualization with sound creates both visual and auditory input. Within modalities, we can identify *sub-modalities*, or individual characteristics that evoke an emotional response. For instance, the visual modality includes such sub-modalities as color vividness and brightness. Auditory modality consists of the volume and pitch of the voice. There are, of course, numerous others. By manipulating sub-modalities, you may change how your subconsciousness reacts to the subject matter. For instance, we pay more attention to vivid bright colors and loud voices, and less attention to subdued colors and low volume.

This allows us to create a program for our subconsciousness. For instance, if we want to remove the negative psychological impact from an event of the past, we can visualize this event on an imaginary TV screen, and then turn down imaginary control knobs to alter the colors and volume, all the way until the visualization shows a blank screen with no sound. This program is interpreted by your subconscious as an instruction to "pay no attention" to the referenced memory. It provides immediate psychological relief, builds self-esteem, and helps in many other ways.

Some of the visualizations are designed to work in the opposite way—to get your subconscious familiar with an imaginary situation and be prepared to act properly in case it is in the driver's seat at the moment. In stressful situations, it is common for the human body to automatically switch into the fight-or-flight mode, which is completely controlled by your subconscious. When you are walking in for your interview, it can easily push your conscious reactions away and put your subconscious in the driver's seat. If you prepare the appropriate programming for your subconscious ahead of time, then it will act exactly as you would consciously—and everything will proceed according to plan.

If the above is not enough, and you still want to learn more, then maybe you should pick an NLP textbook after all—it is a fascinating framework that can change your entire life in many meaningful ways. You may also look up the works of Dr. Joe Dispenza and Dr. Bruce Lipton, who developed their own very powerful methods, unrelated to

NLP, but very helpful to those who prefer a less formal approach to self-development.

APPENDIX III
WHY EATING CALMS YOU DOWN

This is how mammal biology has it: if you are eating, you are likely to be in a safe place. Animals usually get safe cozy before eating. If necessary, they drag their food into their holes or nests or consume it while surrounded by the entire pack. We have the same "hardware" as the other mammalians, and when eating, we subconsciously go off-guard.

There are certain types of foods that can do this better than others. Some of the foods we consider "comfort foods" since our childhood. These are usually the foods cooked in our families when we felt safe at home, and such foods act as lifelong psychological *anchors*—every time we eat them, it feels like in the old days in the childhood.

There are also certain foods that can help calm you down because of their chemical composition. One element that is worth noticing is Magnesium, which has an immediate calming effect on our bodies. There are several magnesium-rich foods readily available, including eggs, spinach, Swiss chard, nuts, seeds, and avocados.